the art of the bath

the art of the bath

SUSANNAH MARRIOTT

MQP

Published by **MQ Publications Limited**
12 The Ivories,
6–8 Northampton Street,
London N1 2HY
Tel: 44 (0) 20 7359 2244
Fax: 44 (0) 20 7359 1616
email: mail@mqpublications.com
website: www.mqpublications.com

Design by **Balley Design Associates**

ISBN: 1 84072 619 9
1 3 5 7 9 0 8 6 4 2

Special thanks to Parker for
music and masala mixes.

Printed and bound in China

Contents

TRIFLES MAKE PERFECTION,
BUT PERFECTION IS NO TRIFLE.

Shaker saying

1

The perfect bath

A ritual of pleasure

The Romans got it right centuries ago. Bathing was a daily necessity whatever your social status (even slaves did it), and included not just the usual skincleansing; it necessitated indulging in massage with scented oils, exfoliation with scrubs, eating, drinking, staring and being stared at, and lots of gossip. Rather like today's spas, then. Bathing occupied so prized a position in Roman society that archeologists have mistaken bathhouses for temples, so fine is the architecture, engineering, and adornment, and so huge the sites.

People have chosen to increase wellbeing by steaming, sweating, or soaking in hot water since long before archeologists have evidence of these practices. The very words for "water" reveal the elemental nature of this tie: the Thai *mae* also signifies "mother," just as a Latin root connects the words *madre*, mother, and *mar*, sea. There is also a long-established link between bathing and spirituality: modern spas may occupy the site of ancient holy wells, the domes of Turkish bathhouses reflect the sacred architecture of the mosque, while the same type of cedarwood is used for both temples and bathhouses in Japan. Bathing and praying are so entwined in Hinduism and Islam that washing is an act of worship.

Perhaps we crave the feel-good sensations of immersion in baths because the human body is some 50–60 percent water. The trappings of modern life—central heating, processed foods, caffeinated drinks—deplete us of water. Consequently, there is a growing spa culture that promises to restore the youthful vitality of well-hydrated skin. A yearning for products that promote natural wellbeing and beauty has led to the rediscovery of traditional treatments that harness the curative powers of water and massage, using recipes concocted from the clays and seaweeds, mineral salts, herbs, and spices native to ancient bathing sites.

The medicinal effects of bathing in hot and cold water—and alternating between the two—are well researched. In a warm bath blood vessels dilate, increasing blood flow away from internal organs to the surface of the skin, and reducing blood pressure. Muscles relax, immune and waste systems get a boost from improved circulation, and tissues receive oxygen and nutrients. Cold water causes blood vessels to constrict, sending blood to the organs to stimulate their functioning. The dash from the overpowering heat of a sauna into an icy forest pool boosts endorphins—natural opiates—and the greater the variance in temperature, the more stimulating the effect. The resulting feeling of euphoric, tingling wellbeing (not to mention fantastic glowing skin) is seriously addictive.

In this book we offer hot soaks and exhilarating showers, exfoliating scrubs and aphrodisiac oils to make your daily bath a ritual of pleasure. As the Romans said, *bene laves*—good bathing.

Water temperature

This is the key to achieving the effect you want: whether your bath is stimulating or soporific depends on water temperature.

Cool bath: 50–75°F/10–24°C—this is stimulating and refreshing, since it causes blood to move toward the internal organs, boosting the workings of the body's systems. Stay in for mere seconds or a couple of minutes.

Tepid bath: 75–85°F/24–30°C—best for a ten-minute morning bath to refresh and restore you for the day ahead.

Warm bath: 85–95°F/30–35°C—deeply relaxing for muscles and mind as blood moves from the organs toward the muscles and skin, improving peripheral circulation. Relax in this heat for more than 15 minutes to gain most benefit.

Hot bath: over 95°F/35°C—good for deep muscular relief and detoxifying perspiration, but can cause faintness and weakness. Best for five minutes only. Avoid if you are pregnant, have varicose veins, or have heart or blood pressure problems.

Drinking water

Sip water to rehydrate the body as you sweat and to combat symptoms as varied as headaches, bad moods, and constipation. Select "mineral" water preferably; this originates from a specific natural source that is constantly monitored. "Spring" water derives from a mix of sources, while "table" water is usually filter-treated faucet water.

Towels and body brushes

"Generous" is the word for luxurious bathtimes: lots of towels, huge enough to envelop the largest person in your household. Choose fluffy cotton—Egyptian cotton is finest—or, like the Japanese, opt for a thinner, smoother fabric that dries quickly, such as crisp cotton waffle or stiff Irish linen. The latter is favored in northern Europe—Finns and Germans like to buff the skin while drying. Choose organic cotton for a clean conscience. Keep to hand a robe, freshly laundered and warmed.

To exfoliate dead skin choose a loofah or long-handled, natural-fiber body brush. Hand mitts can be used with soap for a Turkish steam bath experience; traditional *kese* mitts are very rough. For softer soaping a natural sea sponge is best.

Salt, mud, and herbs

Salt

Sea salt can be used to make a fantastic exfoliating scrub, and mineral salts from spa locations as far afield as Brittany, France, and Japan have been acclaimed for centuries for their curative properties. Try health stores or do a web search for mail order sources of this essential bath ingredient.

Mud

Before bathing, treat yourself to a body or face mask. When clay dries on skin, it draws out impurities and imparts a complex blend of minerals and vitamins that leaves the skin satin-soft. Look for clays from different regions of the world, such as Moroccan rhassoul, white Thai clay, and Dead Sea mud.

Herbs and fruit

Herbal baths are a tried and tested way to absorb the therapeutic properties of herbs. If you don't like the fuss of loose ingredients, opt for single-herb teabags (organic and unbleached). Place the bag in a mug, pour over boiling water, steep for at least ten minutes, remove the bag, and pour the brew into the bath. Alternatively, pile ingredients in a square of muslin, tie, and hang beneath the hot faucet.

Use fresh organic fruit in masks for its antioxidant properties and powerful vitamin punch.

Essential oils

Many bath recipes use essential oils of plants for their intense aroma and therapeutic effect. Never use more drops than recommended—they are highly concentrated. Drop oils onto the surface of bathwater just before stepping in. For massage and bath oils, dilute in a base oil, such as sweet almond or sunflower.

Use only the oils specified, and exercise caution if you are pregnant, breastfeeding, or have high blood pressure, kidney problems, or epilepsy. Some oils cause sensitivity to sunlight: see individual cautions.

HOT WATER: avoid very hot baths if you are pregnant or have varicose veins, and heart or blood pressure problems.

MASSAGE: avoid with fever, high blood pressure, or skin problems. For other health conditions, consult your doctor.

STEAMING: avoid with asthma, respiratory problems, or heart conditions.

SALTS AND SEAWEED: do not use Epsom or mineral salts during pregnancy; avoid seaweed if allergic to iodine.

SCRUBS AND MASKS: avoid full-body exfoliation and masks during pregnancy, with heart or blood pressure problems, and while ill or recovering from illness.

Caution

If you have health concerns, consult your doctor before trying the baths in the book.

THE WAY TO HEALTH IS TO HAVE
AN AROMATIC BATH AND
SCENTED MASSAGE EVERY DAY.

Hippocrates

Luxurious home bathing

FLORAL BATHS

The powerful properties of plants can be made accessible to us by water. These alchemical marvels process the carbon dioxide and nutrients they absorb through various metabolic pathways to produce thousands of new chemicals. To extract these often useful compounds, we need a medium in which the chemicals are soluble. Water is ideal—the hotter it is, the more effective. Essential oils extracted from flowers have been considered the "quintessence", or soul, of the plant by Christian Gnostics, Chinese Taoists, and Arab alchemists alike. Native American healers call up spirits residing in plants to aid healing, while in Bali the flowers cast into baths echo the bowls of floating petals that form part of religious offerings. By adding plants to life-giving water, you help yourself to their ability to lift the spirits, soothe the emotions, and promote positivity.

WHEN YOU FEEL YOURSELF PART OF NATURE
YOU WILL LIVE IN HARMONY.

Tao 13

Rose bath

Native to Iran and in continuous cultivation for more than 3,000 years, the rose has come to symbolize beauty. This "queen of flowers" gives off a lingering, uplifting scent associated with the femininity of Venus; indeed, many consider this the essential oil of choice for women, able to boost self-esteem and sensuality while regulating the menstrual cycle and soothing sensitive skin—Roman ladies made facial preparations from rose petals. Rose is also a symbol of inner beauty, long linked with meditation and rosary beads. What better addition to a calming bath?

Caution: *if pregnant, replace the essential oil with 4 tbsp rosewater.*

INGREDIENTS

handfuls of rose petals (fresh or dried)
10 drops essential oil of rose

chilled rosewater in an atomizer

1 Run a warm bath, strewing the rose petals on the bathwater.

2 Just before stepping in, drop the essential oil into the water and swish with your fingers to disperse.

3 Relax, close your eyes, and turn your focus within to watch your breath moving in and out. Breathe deeply, inhaling the delicious rose scent. Let this erase from your mind all preoccupations as you drift into a meditative state for 10 minutes.

4 Before leaving the bathroom, spritz your face with the rosewater for a refreshing finishing touch.

Lavender bath

Herb of calm and cleanliness, lavender has been strewn on bath water since Roman times to soothe and relax body and mind, and is celebrated for its skin-healing properties. Its very name attests to a longstanding union with bathing culture, deriving from the Latin *lavare*, meaning "to wash." Lavender flowers and essential oil calm, lift the spirits, and reduce muscular tension. In the evening this bath lulls you into deep, restful sleep; in the morning it eases you into the day by refreshing the body and melting a bad mood.

Caution: *omit lavender oil in the first trimester of pregnancy.*

INGREDIENTS

bunch of lavender (fresh or dried)
twine to tie

8 drops essential oil of lavender
crushed lavender flowers (optional)

1 Tie the lavender stalks together with twine and throw the bunch into the water as you run the bath, keeping the water temperature warm in the evening to aid sleep, but cooler in the morning to refresh.

2 If desired, sprinkle the water with crushed lavender flowers.

3 Just before stepping in, drop the essential oil into the water and swish with your fingers to disperse. Relax for 15–20 minutes.

4 Before leaving the bathroom, place a couple of drops of lavender oil on a handkerchief. Inhale during the day when you need instant relaxation.

Sacred springs

Wherever cool or heated water bubbles from the earth, sparkling clean and ever-moving, capable of sustaining life and curing ill-health, mankind has considered the site magical. In Europe Mesolithic finds show natural springs to have been places of settlement and tribute since 5000BCE. The Roman poet Horace thought it proper that springs "more sparkling than glass" should be offered sweet, pure wine and flowers, and even today coins, metal votives, flowers, and strips of cloth are thrown into or adorn wells in an act of petition to bring health and fertility. Over millennia springs were colonized by different belief systems: as the Roman Empire continued to grow, presiding native spirits were overlain with Roman deities, only to be Christianized in their turn, then secularized by Europe's seventeenth- and eighteenth-century spa culture. In the Age of Reason, a spring's healing powers were chemically analyzed, and reattributed from deities to minerals in the water. Today we retreat to urban spas to be enveloped in mineral-rich mud masks and drink oxygenated water in search of eternal youth and wellbeing. In a throwback to their source, some spas overlook sacred springs or holy rivers, and you bathe in pools where pilgrims have always sought spiritual sustenance.

Everywhere in many lands gush forth beneficial waters, here cold, there hot, there both....

Pliny the Elder

Roman postbath massage

Romans, like the Greeks before them, treated bath-softened skin to massage with warm scented oils, a custom still observed in Turkish hammams. Roman cuisine spiked dishes with Eastern-imported flavorings—most popularly ginger, turmeric, and black pepper. Here we include a Roman-style bath with spicy perfumed massage.

Caution: *omit lavender oil in the first trimester of pregnancy.*

INGREDIENTS

2 tbsp sweet almond oil	5 drops essential oil of lavender
5 drops essential oil of black pepper	2 drops essential oil of ginger

1 Heat the room. Mix the oils. Recline in a very warm lavender bath (see page 20) for 20 minutes.

2 Blot yourself dry and sit on a towel. Warm a little oil between your palms.

3 Massage firmly up one calf and thigh, then glide down to the ankle. Build up a rhythm until the oil has been absorbed. Repeat on the other leg.

4 Massage in the same way from wrist to underarm. Circle the shoulder, gliding down the outer arm. Do the other arm.

5 Massage clockwise around your navel with both palms, lifting one over the other. Widen to cover the abdomen.

6 Squeeze and release up your opposite arm, shoulder, and neck. Glide down to repeat. Work on the other side.

Roman bathing

No culture since the Romans has taken the art of bathing to such heights. Wherever they colonized, Romans imported the "civilizing" influence of communal public baths. Spas occupied sites equivalent to many city blocks—the spectacular Caracalla baths in Rome extended over 30 acres. The bathing complex encompassed numerous leisure activities: gyms and libraries, banqueting rooms and gardens, lecture halls and shrines, loungers for sunbathing, corners for gossip and erotic liaisons, places for exfoliation and massage, depilation and dentistry. This was the place to be seen and do business. Women bathed early, men from 2p.m. till dusk each day, whatever their social status, for bathhouses were the people's palaces. And what a bathing tradition they set. The main bathing complex comprised a suite of rooms heated to different temperatures: first the unheated *frigidarium* for a refreshing shower, then the temperate *tepidarium* for scented massage or a sand and olive oil body polish. There followed the hot and humid *caldarium* for steaming and scraping the skin with a metal *strigil* to deep-cleanse, then a hot dip. Then came the hot, dry sauna-like *laconicum*, followed by a cool plunge in curative mineral water.

English country garden bath

Daisies and marigolds, geraniums and lavender…this bath calls on the medicinal powers of the quintessential flowers of the country cottage garden. Marigold is a skin healer, as is camomile, which helps reduce the appearance of dilated veins and skin breakouts. Geranium can enliven a dull complexion and is especially good for rebalancing oily skin. As well as being a valued skin softener, verbena refreshes the spirits with its lemony aroma, and is considered an aphrodisiac. If picking flowers from your garden for this bath, let them infuse in water in the sun for a few hours before use.

Caution: *omit geranium oil during pregnancy and lavender oil in the first trimester.*

INGREDIENTS

2 camomile teabags
2 lemon verbena teabags
handfuls of marigold petals
(fresh or dried)

5 drops essential oil of lavender
3 drops essential oil of geranium

1 Place each teabag in a separate mug and pour over boiling water. Leave to steep for 10 minutes.

2 Run a warm bath, strewing the petals over the water. Place a strainer over the plughole as the water drains.

3 Just before stepping in, pour the teas into the bathwater, then drop in the essential oils and swish to disperse.

4 Relax for 20 minutes or longer, occasionally splashing the floral water over your face.

Japanese blossom bath

Bathing offers Japanese people the opportunity to get closer to nature. Town bathhouses, *sento*, are places of tranquility amid the bustle of urban working life, many opening onto hidden gardens and decorated with images of Mount Fuji. Flowers bring the signature scents and forms of the shifting seasons into the home: cherry blossom signifies April; spring is celebrated with white branches of plum blossom. June, the rainy season, brings the hydrangea and gardenia; winter the waxy camellia. And on special festival days, significant flowers are floated in bathwater.

Caution: *avoid if pregnant, or with varicose veins, heart or blood pressure problems.*

INGREDIENTS

handfuls of seasonal flowers or blossom: orange, cherry, or linden blossom; mimosa, honeysuckle, or jasmine

3 drops essential oil of neroli (bitter orange blossom), linden blossom, or mimosa chilled orange blossom water in an atomizer

1 Run a very hot bath. Strew the flowers over the bathwater. Drop the essential oil into the water bowl of an oil vaporizer, then light the candle beneath it.

2 Scrub the body well (see page 51).

3 Gingerly step into the very hot bath and soak for 10 minutes while inhaling the blossoms' scent. Spritz your face from time to time with the chilled orange blossom water as a cooling antidote to the heat.

Natural bathrooms

Japanese bathhouses were traditionally crafted from fragrant *hinoki* wood, a form of cedar that retains heat well, and when hot and wet suffuses the space with a resiny sweetness. Japanese cypress or Chinese black pine are other options; when wet, both have a sensuous feel and scent. The deep, covered bathtubs and walls, the wooden washing stools, buckets, and ladles would also be hewn from cedar or bamboo. Cedarwood has been used as a temple incense and building material for millennia, as it is thought to generate spiritual strength. The essential oil calms and soothes, rebalancing the nervous system while inducing a state of mind conducive to meditation. Cedarwood oil is also an effective skin softener, with an astringency that helps clear oily skin and benefits the scalp and hair. In Bali *kamar mandi* bathrooms are often open to the sky, sculpted into natural rocks adjoining the home. Ferns grow in the crevices of walls, and fish swim in the deep tank from which you scoop washing water. You shower under blue skies or stars. In both cultures the surroundings of the bathing place ensure that mind and spirit are recharged as you cleanse the body.

Balinese flower bath

In tropical spas beauty treatments end with the ubiquitous Balinese flower bath, awash with the petals of exotic flowers. Among them are heady scented jasmine, ylang ylang, patchouli, hibiscus, and frangipani (waxy blooms from the plumeria, tree so revered that they form part of religious offerings throughout Southeast Asia). If you can't source these flowers locally, improvise with sweet-smelling seasonal blooms from your garden or florist—camellia and rose petals always look attractive.

Caution: *omit jasmine oil during pregnancy.*

INGREDIENTS

handfuls of tropical flowers:
jasmine, ylang ylang, patchouli,
hibiscus, or frangipani
2 drops essential oil of jasmine

2 drops essential oil of ylang ylang
1 drop essential oil of patchouli
1 tbsp sweet almond oil
floral body lotion

1 Run a warm bath, strewing the petals over the bathwater. After the bath, place a strainer over the plughole to catch the petals as the water drains.

2 Drop the essential oils into the sweet almond oil and pour into the bath just before stepping in. Swish to disperse. Close your eyes and luxuriate amid the flowers for 20 minutes or longer.

3 Pat yourself dry and finish by anointing your skin with your favorite floral-scented body lotion.

AROMATIC BATHS

Scent molecules trigger receptor cells behind the bridge of the nose; within seconds information penetrates the olfactory centers in the brain, stimulating the hypothalamus, the part of the brain linked with emotions, mood, and memory. Studies show that inhaling essential oils such as lavender, neroli, and nutmeg can induce feelings of calmness and improve overall wellbeing. In a steamy warm bathroom, scents become more intense, and essential oils (together with their beneficial properties) are absorbed into bath-softened skin more readily. When combined with the instant "letting-go" response to reclining chin-deep in warm water, you can't help but relinquish tension and allow relaxation to engulf you.

THE BEST RECIPE FOR HEALTH IS TO APPLY SWEET SCENTS TO THE BRAIN.

Anacreon, *ancient Greek poet*

Zingy bath

The word "zingy" derives from the Latin name for the ginger plant, *zingiber*. Ginger has extraordinary healing properties. It is hailed as a cure-all in India, China, and Indonesia, and in Europe was thought for centuries to have originated in the Garden of Eden. Golden-hued turmeric is from the ginger family. An antioxidant and anti-inflammatory, capable of reducing the damaging effect of free-radicals on cells, it has held a special place in the beauty lore of India for more than 3,000 years, where it is ubiquitous in masks and scrubs to promote a smooth, clear complexion.

INGREDIENTS

2in (5cm) fresh ginger root
square of muslin and twine to tie
2 tbsp baby rice

½ tsp ground turmeric
2 drops essential oil of ginger

1 Grate the ginger, pile it in the center of the muslin, then tie to secure.

2 Mix together the rice and turmeric, then moisten with water to make a smooth paste.

3 Run a warm bath, hanging the muslin bag beneath the hot faucet.

4 Take handfuls of the paste and massage the body from heels to neck, making circular movements toward the heart to exfoliate the skin. Shower or wash off.

5 Drop the essential oil into the bathwater and swish to disperse before stepping into the bath to relax for 20 minutes.

Minty shower

There is no better early morning refreshment than a blast of peppermint. Guaranteed to rouse you from slumber, this shower gel has a proven ability to promote alertness, detox (by encouraging perspiration), lift headaches, and clear a congested head. It is also good for oily skin. Follow it by massaging the temples with a minty oil; this can be repeated during the day whenever your head feels fuzzy or you need to focus.

Caution: *avoid if you are pregnant or breastfeeding.*

INGREDIENTS

6 drops essential oil of peppermint | **2 tbsp unscented shower gel**

1 Stir the peppermint oil into the unscented shower gel.

2 Mix a minty massage oil using 1 tsp apricot kernel oil and 1 drop essential oil of peppermint and set aside.

3 Step into a tepid shower and massage your body all over with the gel. Brush your skin with a loofah for extra invigoration, making firm strokes toward the heart and paying extra attention to areas of rough skin or cellulite.

4 Turn the heat down to finish with an exhilarating blast of cool water. Stand under for as long as you dare.

5 Blot yourself dry, then dab your index fingers in a little of the minty massage oil and slowly circle the temples to stimulate the brain for the day ahead.

Zesty bath

Citrus oils and fruit are tonics for sluggish skin and sagging spirits. Select your favorite citrus scents, zesting fresh fruit for a bathbag and throwing slices in the tub. Follow with an Indonesian massage oil using peppy lemongrass to enliven exhausted muscles.

Caution: *avoid sunlight for six hours after bathing as citrus oils can cause skin photosensitivity.*

INGREDIENTS

2 unwaxed citrus fruits
square of muslin and twine to tie
5 drops (in total) citrus essential oil:
choose bergamot and neroli to uplift;
or petitgrain and lemon to invigorate; or mandarin and orange to calm and energize; or grapefruit to soothe and revive

1 Zest the fruit using a grater and pile it in the center of the muslin; tie to secure.

2 Slice half the fruit. Mix a massage oil using 1 tbsp each sweet almond and coconut oils and 6 drops essential oil of lemongrass.

3 Run a warm bath, hanging the muslin bag beneath the hot faucet. Slice one fruit and scatter into the bathwater.

4 Just before stepping in, drop the essential oils into the bathwater and swish to disperse. Luxuriate in the reviving scents.

5 Pat yourself dry. Warm a little of the mixed massage oil between your palms and massage the arm and leg muscles with smooth sweeping strokes toward the heart. Knead and pummel tense areas, then finish with fingertip strokes.

Exotic bath

The heavenly combination of coconut and vanilla used for beauty treatments in the Maldives is the inspiration for this bath. No part of the coconut, considered a fruit of the gods in India, is wasted in Asian beauty treatments. The finely grated flesh is blended with spices such as turmeric to exfoliate and nourish the skin; the husk tackles dry skin on the feet; the milk makes a softening bath. Vanilla adds a fragrance shown in research trials to lessen anxiety and induce relaxation.

INGREDIENTS

1 coconut   3 vanilla pods

1 Split the coconut and remove the flesh. Grate it, cover with warm water, and allow to steep. Blend in a food processor, then place in a strainer over a bowl. Press the flesh with the back of a spoon to extract the milk. Place a vanilla pod in the milk and leave to infuse.

2 Run a warm bath, strewing the rest of the vanilla pods over the bathwater.

3 Massage the body from heels to neck, working toward the heart, with handfuls of coconut flesh, concentrating on areas of rough skin. Wipe off with a warm, wet washcloth.

4 Before stepping into the bath, pour in the coconut milk. Enjoy the silky sensation and scented water. After the bath, dry out the vanilla pods for reuse.

Spicy bath

Sweet but biting, this bath mix brings a tingle to the toes. It is based on an invigorating combination of cinnamon, cardamom, cloves, coriander, and cumin that resembles Indian cuisine's masala blends. The cinnamon tree is one of the oldest recorded plants with an aromatic use. India's queen of spices, cardamom, is uplifting and refreshing, while cloves stimulate the senses and release muscle tension. Coriander cleanses and cools the skin and relieves nervous tension.

Caution: *omit cinnamon and cloves and their oils during pregnancy.*

INGREDIENTS

I cinnamon stick, broken
I tsp cumin seeds
I tsp cloves
I tsp cardamom

square of muslin and twine to tie
2 drops essential oil of coriander
2 drops essential oil of clove

1 Whizz the spices in a coffee grinder, pile on the muslin, then tie to secure.

2 Run a hot bath, hanging the muslin bag beneath the hot faucet.

3 Drop the coriander and orange oils into the water and swish to disperse;

drop the clove oil into the water bowl of an oil vaporizer, then light the candle.

4 Step into a double hit of invigoration—heat and spiciness—for 15 minutes.

5 Pat dry. Don a robe and lie down for a while, taking occasional sips of water.

Fruity bath

Fruit is as good for skin as it is to eat. Buff the body with pureed papaya, then recline in a bath with a watermelon facemask. The skin of the antioxidant-rich papaya contains a rich concentration of the enzyme papain, shown to revitalize the complexion. It is a natural source of alphahydroxy acid and is prized for exfoliating without irritating. Watermelon has a clarifying effect on skin, and in India it is considered the most cooling mask to combat summer heat.

INGREDIENTS

1 slice watermelon
1 ripe mango, peeled and chopped
1 banana, peeled and chopped

1 slice pineapple, peeled and cored
1 ripe papaya

1 To make the facemask, grate the watermelon into a strainer over a bowl. Press with the back of a spoon to force the juice into the bowl. Set aside for later use.

2 Juice the mango, banana, and pineapple; pour into a glass to make a refreshing drink to enjoy during your bath. Halve and deseed the papaya. Scoop out the flesh and purée it. Reserve the skins.

3 Run a tepid bath. Massage the puréed papaya from heels to shoulders. Shower or wash off immediately.

4 Relax in the bath, sipping the juice. Massage the insides of the papaya skins over your face and neck for 2 minutes. Alternatively, apply the watermelon mask: soak cotton balls in the juice and wipe your face and neck. Relax for 15 minutes; splash with hot, then cool, water.

Creativity bath

More than a few inventors—from Archimedes on—have had their best ideas in the bath. As you lie back and switch off, the mind is freed to set off on flights of fancy, and solutions to problems seem to emerge effortlessly. Certain aromas are thought to promote creativity: choose a blend that appeals from the next page to scent your bathwater. Sip peppermint tea to stimulate the brain further—the brain is 85 percent water and its cells send messages more readily in a well-hydrated medium. Keep a pen and paper to hand.

1 Run a tepid bath. Just before stepping in, pour the oil blend into the bathwater and swish to disperse.

2 Lie back, close your eyes, and switch your mind away from everyday matters by focusing on your breathing. Watch your breath move in and out.

3 When unwelcome thoughts arise, notice them, ask them to leave, then return to awareness of your breathing. If it helps, imagine intrusive thoughts as clouds moving across a blue sky. Do this for at least 10 minutes.

4 When bright ideas surface, jot them down; try not to soak the paper! If the bathwater gets too cold, run in a little hot water.

5 After stepping out of the bath, rub your body vigorously with a towel to stimulate mind and body further.

Bath oils to boost creativity

Caution: *omit melissa and myrrh oils during pregnancy; avoid strong sunlight for at least six hours after bathing.*

 ### CITRUS OIL BLEND

3 drops essential oil of lemon
(to bring about clear thinking and
boost circulation)

1 drop essential oil of lime
(to counter apathy)
1 drop essential oil of melissa (to remove
mental blocks and instill positivity)

SPICED OIL BLEND

3 drops essential oil of coriander
(to stimulate a tired mind and
boost memory)

2 drops essential oil of cardamom
(to clear away confused thoughts and
energize jaded senses)
1 drop essential oil of ginger (to sharpen
the senses and memory)

EXOTIC OIL BLEND

2 drops essential oil of palmarosa
(to bring clarity to a subject)
2 drops essential oil of patchouli
(for clear thinking and objectivity)

2 drops essential oil of myrrh
(to lift apathy)

DETOXIFYING BATHS

At certain times of year—after the excesses of the winter festivals, with the onset of summer and the thought of bikinis, before a wedding—many of us feel the need to "detoxify" the body, eating healthily, taking an exercise regimen seriously, and sloughing away dead skin cells to leave face and body glowing and radiant. Here are exfoliation and anticellulite spa treatments, hangover bath cures, and deep-cleansing treats using some of nature's most potent skin healers: mud, salt, tonic herbs, and seaweed. There are revitalizing showers, too, which harness the energy of moving water: the negative ions in fine droplets of water will help revive those who feel physically and emotionally lethargic.

Pouring warm water over the body bestows strength….

Ashtanga Hridayam 2:17

Prebath body brushing

There is no more effective way to exfoliate dead cells, tone the skin, combat cellulite, and stimulate the senses, than to brush all over with the dry bristles of a natural bristled body brush before stepping into a bath or shower. By boosting circulation and encouraging the elimination of toxins, this is valued for strengthening the immune system. As you brush, pay special attention to areas of the body where the skin is dry or neglected: the elbows and heels, knees and buttocks, thighs and upper arms perhaps.

Caution: *avoid if you have an infection, heart or blood pressure problems, or cancer.*

1 First make sure that your skin is dry. Start brushing at your feet and work up the back then the front of your legs. Use long, brisk, circular strokes, ensuring that you always work toward the heart.

2 Repeat the stroke on the back and front of the arms, then turn your attention to the buttocks.

3 Work over the abdominal area, circling in a clockwise direction to stimulate the digestive system.

4 Brush as far over your shoulders and upper back as you can easily reach.

5 Finish by gently sweeping over your décolletage, working with care over the delicate skin, and avoiding the breasts.

Hangover bath

When you can hardly crawl out of bed after over-doing it the night before, ask someone to run you a bath, then drop in plant oils that help reduce nausea and headaches, clear away fugginess, soothe aching muscles, and boost your damaged sense of wellbeing. Sip mineral water or peppermint tea as you try to relax.

INGREDIENTS

2 drops essential oil of grapefruit
2 drops essential oil of peppermint
4 drops essential oil of marjoram

small bag of frozen peas
chilled gel eye mask or 2 cooled
  camomile teabags

1 Drag yourself to the bathroom and run a tepid bath—this water temperature will help revive you.

2 Drop the essential oils into the water and swish to disperse. Step in.

3 Fold a hand towel around the bag of frozen peas and use it to cushion the back of your head.

4 Close your eyes and put on the chilled gel eye mask. Alternatively, place a camomile teabag over each eyelid. Relax until you feel you can face the world again.

5 If your headache lingers once you leave the bath, gently rub a drop of undiluted essential oil of lavender into your temples using your index finger.

Sea salt bath

Associated with purity and immortality by the Romans, salt comprises the very components we need for life—sodium and chlorine. Seaweed is strongly antioxidant, contains the invaluable nutrients iodine and selenium, and its constituent polysaccharides help stimulate immunity. It is also one of the richest sources of vitamin B12, potassium, calcium, and iron. This bath calls on the powers of these wonder substances to deep-cleanse and nourish.

Caution: *avoid if you are pregnant, or have heart or blood pressure problems.*

INGREDIENTS

2 large strips kombo or nori seaweed
20 tbsp sea salt, finely ground

2 limes, freshly sliced

1 Place the seaweed in a large pan, cover well with water, bring to the boil, and simmer for 20 minutes, lidded.

2 Run a tepid bath, then add half the salt and the lime slices.

3 Step into the shower and moisten the body with tepid water. Massage the body with handfuls of salt, from heels to shoulders, using extensive circular movements toward the heart. Shower off, gradually making the water cooler.

4 Strain the seaweed liquid into the bath, then relax in it for 10 minutes. Run in cold water; take it as cool as you dare.

5 Finish with another cool shower to wash away any traces of salt.

Steam bathing

Steaming as a method of deep-cleansing the skin seems to have been part of most cultures in the past: archeologists have unearthed evidence of sweatbaths for communal bathing from Ireland and Lapland in northern Europe to the *temezcal* vapor bath of Mayan Mexico and Guatemala. Sweating not only cools the body, it is one of its most efficient detoxification processes. When the body is subjected to heat, blood vessels in the skin dilate and sweat glands produce perspiration. The increased blood flow promotes an exchange between the blood and skin tissue: waste products in the blood pass out to skin cells to be eliminated as the skin takes up nutrients and oxygen from the blood.

Before the mass availability of soap, perspiring skin made for much more efficient cleansing and moisturizing than water alone could offer.

The best-known form of steam bath is probably the Turkish hammam. Here, surrounded by the domes of Islamic architecture and intricate tilework, you relax to sweat on a hot marble "navel stone" in misty, eucalyptus-scented heated rooms, lulled by the sound of water running into marble basins. After a period of relaxation comes a powerful scrubbing and soaping, followed by vigorous massage with oil, before finishing with a cold-water splash or lounge in a cool room, rehydrating with a glass of sweetened mint tea.

THE SWEAT LODGE UTILIZES ALL POWERS OF THE UNIVERSE: EARTH, AND THINGS THAT GROW FROM THE EARTH; WATER, FIRE, AND AIR.

Black Elk, *Native American Ogola-Dakota holy man*

Facial steaming

Steaming the face brings to skin the benefits of a full-body steaming, and is easy to do at home once a week. When you add essential oils to the steam, the heat helps the skin absorb their curative powers more rapidly; it also makes the steam aromatic. Applying moisturizer to still-damp skin traps in steamy moisture for that plump, youthful look. Steam facials also help clear blocked sinuses, relax the muscles of the chest, neck, and shoulders, and deepen the breathing for complete relaxation.

Caution: *avoid if you have asthma, or respiratory or heart problems.*

INGREDIENTS

2 drops essential oil of sandalwood   1 drop essential oil of frankincense

1 Remove makeup and cleanse the skin thoroughly. Drop the essential oils into a basin of recently boiled water.

2 Place your face about 10in (25cm) from the basin and drape a towel over your head and the bowl.

3 Remain under this tent for 5–10 minutes. Breathe through your nose to clear your sinuses.

4 For deeper breathing that promotes calmness, inhale slowly through your mouth for a count of 4, hold the breath for 4, then exhale for 4. Repeat for up to 2 minutes.

5 Remove the towel, pat your face dry, and apply moisturizer immediately.

Cleansing the soul

"There is no dirt in Heaven," stated Mother Ann Lee (1736–84), founder of the Shakers, echoing a theme running through many faith traditions—that cleanliness is next to godliness. For Muslims, being in the state of *wudu*, ritual cleanliness, restores mankind's original state of perfection, and is a condition for *salat*, prayer. So, five times a day, you purify the body in fresh running water as a prerequisite for standing before God to cleanse the soul. Before a religious vision quest, Crow Indians take a ritual sweatbath, cutting wood for a fire to heat stones, burning sweet cedar branches for incense, and sitting naked in darkness to be purified by the elements of fire, water, and earth in preparation for a time of spiritual searching. Other Native American religions alternate this with plunging into an icy river. Zen monks affirm "I must cleanse my body and my heart" before bathing, attending to ritual ablutions with focus, using the rhythm of repetition and mindfulness of the breath to enter fully into the present and cleanse the mind of other thoughts while undertaking this most mundane but holy of daily tasks.

The key to Paradise is *salat* and the key to *salat* is *wudu* or ablution.

Prophet Muhammad

Thorough soaping

A traditional hammam treatment is here adapted for the privacy of your own bathroom: choose soap rich in olive oil to nourish the skin. Japanese bathers also vigorously scrub with soap, seeing washing and bathing as separate activities. Every fraction of the body is scoured energetically, then scoops of water are thrown over the head to slosh away suds before bathers inch into a fantastically hot bath.

Caution: *avoid if you are pregnant or have varicose veins, heart or blood pressure problems.*

 INGREDIENTS

lavender and olive oil soap ⋮ hand mitt

1 Run a very hot bath, allowing steam to fill the room. In the shower build up a lather from top to toe with lashings of soap. Let the suds rest on your skin for a few minutes as the olive oil is absorbed.

2 Rub all over with the rough mitt, making long, deep sweeps toward the heart followed by small up-and-down movements for very deep cleansing.

3 Wash your hair, moving the skin on your scalp as you shampoo.

4 Rinse off the soap suds and dead skin in a warm shower, turning the dial to cool for a moment.

5 Step into the deep, hot bath and feel steam opening your pores as you relax into the soothing warm water.

Mud bath

Rich in minerals and trace elements, clay dries on the skin, absorbing impurities and excess oil. As it tightens, blood is drawn to the surface, boosting circulation. Mud also retains heat, making the body sweat, which only boosts the purifying effect and better permits the exchange of organic compounds into the tissue. Perform this treatment in a hot bathroom: shut the door before turning on the faucet to keep the room steamy.

Caution: *avoid if you are pregnant, or have heart or blood pressure problems.*

 **INGREDIENTS**

1 pack body mud: mix as instructed
8 drops essential oil of eucalyptus

washcloth chilled in a basin of iced water

1 Heat the room. Fill the tub with extremely hot water. Drop the essential oil into the water-filled bowl of an oil vaporizer, then light the candle underneath it.

2 Stand on a large towel and massage the mud from feet to neck. Relax for 15 minutes, rubbing in the mud as you perspire and inhaling the herbal fumes. If

you become too hot, mop your brow with the washcloth, and sip a glass of chilled mineral water.

3 Shower off the mud. Check the bath temperature and add cold water if necessary, then soak.

4 Pat yourself dry, don a bathrobe, and relax for 20 minutes, sipping water.

Russian baths

Russia's traditional *banya*, or bathhouse, uses deep heat and steam to cleanse the body. The extreme humidity speeds up the detoxification processes, while skin and muscles are further stimulated with massage: pounding with a *veynik* or leafy twig brings blood to the surface, reddening the skin. After showering to wash away outdoor grime, you enter the *parilka*, or interior room, intensely hot, with a furnace of hot rocks at its epicenter. When steam is produced from playing water onto the rocks, it can become hard to breathe or even to expose skin. Then you submit to a beating from the pine or birch swatches which stir the hot air and set up a rhythmic swish over feet, limbs, back and front. After cooling in a plunge pool, you may return to the intense heat. Banyas are often constructed from dark wood, and a forest-like scent fills the space as the leaves macerate in buckets of warm water; the same process is used before distillation of oil from the tree bark— soaking frees the essential oil. Birch oil is thought to ward off evil spirits; more practically, it helps chronic skin conditions.

THE BANYA IS YOUR SECOND MOTHER.

Russian saying

Sauna

The essence of the prehistoric Finnish sauna is dry heat. This encourages circulation within the skin, deep relaxation of muscles and mind, and detoxifying perspiration. You boost circulation and exfoliation by "whisking" the body with a *vihta* or *vasta*, a bunch of young leafy twigs of birch, cedar, or pine. When a ladle of water is played onto the hot stones, it sends up *löyly*, searing steam, the spirit of the sauna (the word signifies not just vapor, but breath, or soul). The profound nature of a sauna is enhanced by a window looking out onto nature, for silent contemplation. When too hot, participants dash into a pool of icy water or sit in the chill open air; the contrast between hot and cold brings about an almost euphoric sense of wellbeing. Saunas are constructed from pine or fir, both of which, when heated, emit a resiny scent that helps the cleansing process. Essential oil of fir stimulates the respiratory system, alleviating chest conditions and asthma. It is a tonic for the nervous system, too, and its warming action eases tired, aching limbs. Detoxifying and refreshing, pine oil stimulates the organs that process waste products. The original smoke sauna, *savusauna*, was wood-heated, so was smokily scented.

In the sauna you must conduct yourself as in church.

Finnish saying

Home sauna

Run a hot, steamy bath, carefully place two just-boiled kettles on the bathroom floor, lids removed or open, and heat 3 drops of essential oil of fir or pine into the water of an oil vaporizer. Wash with pine-scented soap. If you can light a woodfire in the bathroom, infuse the logs with up to 12 drops of essential oil. The aroma of pine refreshes, and has long been used to help ease respiratory and sinus conditions: in the past, people retreated to clean-scented pine forests to relieve pulmonary disease. Enhance your contemplative soaking with yoga breathing (see below).

Caution: *avoid if you are pregnant, or have varicose veins, heart or blood pressure problems.*

1 Fold your right index and middle fingers into your palm. Rest your ring and little fingers on your left nostril, thumb on your right nostril.

2 Inhale through both nostrils, block your left nostril with your ring and little fingers, and exhale through your right nostril. Inhale through your right nostril.

3 At the top of the inhalation, block your right nostril with your thumb, release your ring and little fingers, and exhale through your left nostril. Inhale through your left nostril. Repeat for two minutes. Finish on an exhalation from the right nostril, then inhale through both nostrils.

Japanese New Year bath

New Year in Japan, *Ko Shogatsu*, is the time for spring cleaning, when homes are redolent with resiny pine branches. At this season of renewal and regeneration, it makes sense to cleanse the body, too. Pine is an excellent restorative to add to bathwater, and the needles have a tonic effect. Sprouts from young pine, larch, fir, or juniper trees, make a more stimulating mix. Infuse them in boiling water for 20 minutes, then strain the water into the bath. Essential oil of pine has a detoxifying action on the kidneys, gallbladder, and adrenal glands. It boosts circulation and sweating, is healing for skin and lung conditions, and refreshes the mind. Alternatively, follow the ancient tradition from some parts of England and brave a dip in the sea on New Year's Day.

Caution: *avoid if you are pregnant, or have varicose veins, heart or blood pressure problems.*

INGREDIENTS

handfuls of pine needles
square of muslin and twine to tie

6 drops essential oil of pine

1 Pile the pine needles in the center of the muslin, then tie to secure. Run a hot bath, hanging the muslin bag beneath the hot faucet.

2 Give yourself a good scrub with a hard mitt (see page 51).

3 Just before stepping into the bath, drop the essential oil into the water and swish to disperse. Relax for 10–15 minutes.

4 Pat yourself dry, don a bathrobe, and lie down for 20 minutes, sipping a glass of cool mineral water.

Skin-shining shower

Sesame seeds and honey form the basis of this skin-softening exfoliation paste which will impart a silky sheen to the skin. Rich in unsaturated fat, protein, vitamins and minerals, sesame seeds are extremely nutritious for the skin, and were being used to beautify and heal as far back as the time of the Ancient Egyptians. Honey is a wonder food for the skin, with a powerful ability to zap cell-damaging free radicals and, as a natural humectant, to seal in moisture. Mint adds extra zing.

Caution: *avoid during pregnancy.*

INGREDIENTS

4 tbsp black sesame seeds
2 tsp dried mint

8 tbsp runny honey

1 Mix the ingredients to make a paste. Take handfuls of the paste and massage the body from your feet up to your neck, making small circular movements toward the heart. Work slowly so the treatment lasts a full 15 minutes.

2 Place a strainer over the plughole, then shower or wash away the sticky paste. Feel how silky your skin is.

3 Mix a sesame-mint body oil using 2 tbsp sesame oil, 6 drops essential oil of lavender, 3 drops essential oil of benzoin, and 1 drop essential oil of peppermint and apply liberally.

Body-polishing treatment

In Java women of the court would traditionally be given a daily spicy *lulur* body rub to smooth, exfoliate, and scent the skin. Brides received the pampering treat for forty days before a wedding. This *lulur* blend includes ginger and turmeric for their stimulating, deep-cleansing, antioxidant, and regenerative properties. Follow the treatment with a tropical floral bath. In Indonesia they say this is the way to enter heaven.

Caution: *avoid during pregnancy.*

 INGREDIENTS

4 tbsp baby rice
4 tsp ground ginger
4 tsp ground sandalwood

1 tsp ground turmeric
8 drops essential oil of jasmine
large tub of live natural yogurt

1 Mix the rice and spices, then, drop by drop and constantly stirring, add enough water to make a smooth paste. Stir in the jasmine oil.

2 Rub the paste over your skin, working up from feet to neck.

3 Let the paste dry, then stand on a large towel and, using your fingertips, make circular movements all over the skin to rub off the dried body mask.

4 Shower or wash, then coat skin with the yogurt to cool and soften it. Shower or wash again. Don't worry if your skin has a golden glow: it will fade.

5 Run a deep, warm Balinese Flower Bath (see page 29), and relax for 20 minutes.

Anticellulite shower

This treatment combines a deeply detoxifying scrub with pounding water jets to increase circulation in areas of rough, dimpled flesh. The black pepper scrub calls on the penetrating heat and stimulating energy of this "king of spices." Applied to the skin, pepper dilates blood vessels to boost circulation and heats muscles while offering a nutritious mix of protein and minerals. According to Ayurveda, one of the oldest systems of medicine on earth, which originated in India, black pepper burns *ama*, toxins. Cedarwood promotes circulation, too, while cypress works on fluid retention.

Caution: *avoid during pregnancy.*

INGREDIENTS

2 tbsp sea salt, finely ground
2 tsp freshly ground black pepper
2 tbsp olive oil

1 drop essential oil of cedarwood
3 drops essential oil of cypress

1 Mix the ingredients to make a scrub, set aside, then take a refreshing shower.

2 Massage handfuls of the scrub onto damp skin. Work up the inner and outer thighs and around the buttocks with large circular strokes, then kneading movements to lift and squeeze the flesh.

3 If desired, brush with a loofah. After 15 minutes, wipe away the scrub with a warm, wet washcloth.

4 Take a cool shower, directing the jet at your buttocks and thighs. Make small circles, turning the pressure up and temperature down. Towel dry vigorously.

Anticellulite self-massage

Follow an invigorating shower with a spot treatment for the hips and buttocks. This oil blend combines juniper for its detoxifying action and ability to act on fluid retention, astringent rosemary to stimulate and reduce puffiness, and lavender to soothe and rebalance the skin, all enveloped in sesame oil to help diminish stretch marks. Work on one side, then the other.

Caution: *omit juniper and rosemary oils during pregnancy and lavender in the first trimester.*

 **INGREDIENTS**

2 tbsp sesame oil
2 drops essential oil of juniper

2 drops essential oil of rosemary
2 drops essential oil of lavender

1 Mix all the oils. Kneeling on a towel, warm a little oil between your palms. Make long, smooth palm strokes up from one knee, and around the buttocks and hips, then glide down.

2 Using the "V" of one hand (between thumb and index finger), scoop up flesh on the inner thigh, lift, and release into the "V" of your other hand. Knead like this up the inner, then the outer legs.

3 Stand up, make loose fists, and pummel the buttocks.

4 With the knuckles of one hand, then the other, rotate up the front and back of the thighs, then around the buttocks.

5 Finish with smooth, flowing palm strokes from knee to hip at the front and back of one leg. Repeat the movement for the other leg.

Indian bathing

Water is the source and the place to which we should return, the Hindu holy scriptures teach. Rivers are the veins of Mother Earth, and *ghat*, steps leading to the edge, are a crossing point between heaven and earth, making them places for worship. That water is the essence of everything, predating life, is echoed in the first words of the Bible. Before God creates light, earth and heaven, sun and stars and all is formless, there is water. The daily *puja*, prayer ritual that invokes the divine, is preceded by bathing, the first act of the day to purify soul and body ready to receive the divine. Most auspicious is to bathe in a sacred river, submerging three times while repeating *mantras*, sacred formulae. Water—considered liquid energy—is scooped between cupped palms as you invoke the deities and make oblation to the rising sun; here the energies of two life-giving forces meet. Use your own morning bath to cleanse your spirit, taking a few minutes to focus on the image of the rising sun and the hope it embodies.

And the Spirit of God moved upon the face of the waters.

Genesis 1:2

PAMPERING BATHS

Here are beautifying baths for those forgotten areas of the body: soaks to soften dry feet and polish unkempt hands; deep-heat treatments to silken lacklustre hair; and intense moisture baths for dry, sensitive skin. Postbath massages complete the pampering experience—there are pressure-point treatments for aching feet, soothing strokes to restore hands and nails, and Indian oil baths for all-over silky softness. Seclude yourself in the bathroom and emerge a new woman.

WOMEN ARE AT THEIR MOST BEAUTIFUL ONE HOUR AFTER THE SAUNA.

Finnish saying

Softening foot soak

Let buckets of water bring relief to calves, shins, feet, and toes—particularly soothing after wearing high heels. Fill one bucket—a large plastic bin would be even better—with very hot water, another with cold water. Add a therapeutic herbal solution (see below), sit back, and relax.

Caution: *avoid rosemary and peppermint oils if you are pregnant or breastfeeding, and rosemary and eucalyptus oils if you have high blood pressure or epilepsy.*

1 Sit on a chair and sink both legs in the hot water to the knees for 10 minutes.

2 Very quickly plunge both legs into the cold water. Try to bear it for 2 minutes—scream out loud if you must.

3 Return your legs to the hot water bath for another 10 minutes. Finish with a quick cool plunge before drying your tinglingly fresh feet.

THERAPEUTIC ADDITIONS FOR HOT FOOTBATHS

4 drops essential oil of clary sage
(for itchy, sweating feet)
4 drops essential oil of eucalyptus
(to revive feet and legs)
4 drops essential oil of peppermint
(to relieve irritating itchy and
inflamed skin)

4 drops essential oil of rosemary
(for aching, swollen feet)
1 cup of long-brewed green tea
(for tired feet)
1 tbsp mustard powder mixed to a paste
with a little water (for painful,
swollen feet)

Shiatsu footbath

You can buy *tsunami* mats to activate acupressure points on the feet as you stand in the shower. As an alternative, fill a large flat-bottomed plastic bowl with a layer of different-sized pebbles and top up with cool water. As a tonic after work, step into the bowl and trample the pebbles. This is another good antidote to the consequences of wearing high heels.

Caution: *omit peppermint and rosemary oils during pregnancy, and rosemary oil if you have high blood pressure or epilepsy.*

INGREDIENTS

1 tbsp sweet almond oil	3 drops essential oil of peppermint
1 tbsp coconut oil	3 drops essential oil of rosemary
1 tsp runny honey	

1 Sit on a chair with a footbath by your feet. Activate your energy by tapping the sole of your left foot with your fingertips from the base of the toes to the heel. Repeat on the right foot.

2 Plunge both feet into the cool water. When accustomed to the temperature, stand up, holding onto a table or chair for stability. Step up and down, exerting pressure on each part of the foot in turn. Where it feels painful, ease down gently before shifting your weight. Tread on sharper gravel as well as smooth pebbles, appreciating the range of sensations.

3 After 5 minutes, dry your feet. Mix the ingredients and massage into the feet.

Nail repair bath

This bedtime treat for ravaged hands and nails leaves them smooth and youthful-looking. After the massage, put on cotton gloves and go to bed.

Caution: *omit jasmine oil during pregnancy.*

INGREDIENTS

1 tbsp sesame oil
1/2 tbsp sweet almond oil
1/2 tbsp avocado oil
3 drops essential oil of lavender
3 drops essential oil of jasmine

3 drops essential oil of sandalwood
1 vitamin E capsule
1/2 lemon, juice only
1 tsp avocado oil

1 Mix an intensive care oil using the sesame, almond, and avocado oils, essential oils and vitamin E, pricking the capsule to squeeze out the contents.

2 Fill a bowl with warm water, adding the lemon juice and avocado oil. Soak hands for 2–3 minutes. Pat dry.

3 Pour a few drops of the oil blend into one palm. Supporting that palm with the fingers of the other hand, circle the middle of the palm with the thumb of the supporting hand. Circle wider.

4 Turn the hand over and slide the thumb from the base of the fingers to the wrist.

5 Massage the digits from base to tip between your thumb and index finger. Squeeze to pull away. Repeat on the other hand.

Skin-soothing oatmeal bath

The milky softness that oats bring to a bath is incredibly healing to itchy, irritated skin. Lavender and camomile augment the palliative powers of oatmeal: lavender promotes new cell growth, while camomile reduces puffiness and strengthens skin tissue. If possible, choose oatmeal from an organic source.

Caution: *omit camomile and lavender oil in the first trimester of pregnancy.*

 INGREDIENTS

2 tbsp dried oatmeal
square of muslin and twine to tie

5 drops essential oil of lavender
5 drops essential oil of camomile

1 Pile the oatmeal in the center of the muslin, then tie to secure. Run a tepid bath, hanging the muslin bag beneath the faucet as the bath fills.

2 Just before stepping in, drop the essential oils into the water and swish to disperse. Relax in the bath for at least 20 minutes for full therapeutic effect.

3 Let the muslin bag dry out for use again the next day. Discard after using it a couple of times.

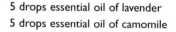

Conditioning hair soak

In Indonesian spas hair treatments almost always include a cream hair bath. This home-spa version uses scented oils to tone the hair and scalp. For best results, relax in a floral bath for 20 minutes while they take effect.

Caution: *avoid rosemary, jasmine, and geranium oils during pregnancy, and rosemary oil if you have high blood pressure or epilepsy.*

INGREDIENTS

6 drops (total) essential oils: ylang ylang, rosemary, or jasmine (to rejuvenate and stimulate circulation); or lavender or geranium (to balance oil production); or sandalwood (to nourish dry hair)

2 tbsp unscented conditioner for your hair type

1 Stir the oils into the conditioner. Run a warm floral bath (see pages 16–29).

2 Wash your hair, rinse, then smother it with the creamy solution, moving the scalp with your fingertips.

3 Cover your hair with a shower cap and recline in the bath.

4 Imagine taking oxygen to the scalp. Inhale slowly through your nose for a count of 4, hold for 4, then exhale for 4. Take a regular breath if necessary. Repeat for 2–3 minutes. As you become confident extend the outbreath to 8 counts.

5 Rinse your hair in warm, then cool, running water.

Deeply moisturizing bath

This opulent oil bath will leave your skin in top condition. While you relax in it, apply a weekly rich facemask; it works best at night. Honey has been hailed as a powerful skin healer from the ancient world to modern hospitals. Packed with properties that fight free radicals, it is a humectant that attracts moisture to cells and starves bacteria. Almonds, a creamily soothing skin food, have been a symbol of allure in India since Mughal times: Ayurvedic philosophy states that these nuts build *ojas*, life sap.

Caution: *omit rosemary, geranium, and jasmine oils during pregnancy.*

INGREDIENTS

2 tbsp sweet almond oil
2 tsp wheatgerm oil
6 drops essential oils of rose

6 drops essential oils of geranium
4 drops essential oil of jasmine
1 vitamin E capsule

1 Mix a rich facemask using 2 tsp runny honey, 2 tsp fresh cream, 2 tsp ground almonds and 6 drops essential oil of frankincense stirring well. Set aside.

2 Blend the oils and pour half into a warm bath just before stepping in. Swish to disperse.

3 Pat the mask over your face and neck, avoiding the eyes and mouth. Allow to dry for 20 minutes.

4 Gently rub off the mask, using small fingertip circles. Splash with warm water.

5 Pat dry. Massage in the remaining oil.

Postbath self–massage

After a bath is the perfect time for a massage, or Ayurvedic "oil bath," because the skin is soft and the oil seals in moisture. You will need 2 tbsp oil, such as sweet almond or sunflower; apply more whenever necessary.

1 Warm some oil between your palms. Sandwiching one foot between your hands, stroke your thumbs up the sole and out in a T-shape. Do the same with the other foot.

2 Stroke the lower leg from ankle to knee, then glide down. Firmly stroke front and back thighs from knee to hip, gliding down. Repeat on the other leg.

3 Knead your buttocks and hips. Then place your hands on your waist, on either side of the spine. Smooth your palms down, out over the hips, and around to the starting point. Repeat.

4 Circle the navel clockwise with both palms, lifting one hand over the other as they meet and widening the stroke to cover the abdomen.

5 With one hand, squeeze and release down the other side of your neck and across the shoulders. Repeat on the other side with the other hand.

6 Float one hand down your other arm, and massage firmly up the lower and upper arms, releasing over the elbow. Cup the palm and cover it with short, sliding thumb strokes. Repeat on the other arm and hand.

RELAXING BATHS

Baths can be blissfully comforting: weightless and enveloped in warmth, you feel safe and nurtured, and stress evaporates. Paint your bathroom in relaxing shades of light green and pale blue, off-white and dove grey—the colors of the moon, the planet thought to preside over this part of the home in the Indian tradition of Vastu, often referred to as Indian feng shui. In honor of the moon, place mirrors on the northern and eastern walls, and follow the recommendations in the ancient Hindu text *The Mayamata*, filling your bathing space with plants, flowers, and fine fragrances.

Health requires this relaxation,
The aimless life,
This life in the present.

Henry David Thoreau

Postworkout bath

Ease overworked muscles with a long, hot soak. Finish with a massage using a warming, pain-relieving oil blend: juniper oil contains myrcene, an analgesic.

Caution: *avoid if you are pregnant, or have high blood pressure, epilepsy, or kidney disease.*

INGREDIENTS

4 drops essential oil of rosemary
3 drops essential oil of marjoram

2 drops essential oil of ginger

1 Run a very warm bath. Mix a postworkout massage oil blend using 2 tbsp sunflower oil and 10 drops juniper oil and set aside.

2 Drop the essential oils into the water and swish to disperse. Rest your weary bones for 20 minutes or so. Try not to ponder disappointments. As you relax, visualize making the perfect return of serve or scoring the goal of the season.

3 Pat yourself dry, then warm a little massage oil between your palms, and make firm sweeping strokes with alternate palms up one calf. Glide down the leg and repeat the stroke, building a rhythm.

4 Place knuckles or a thumb over a tense area in the calf, press, and circle. Glide to another area and repeat, gradually covering the whole muscle. Finish with long soothing strokes.

5 Repeat on the other calf, the thighs, biceps, and triceps, then knead the neck and shoulders.

Aching muscles bath

Use the healing powers of herbs and hot water to relieve aching muscles and stiff joints, as soothing scents bring about total body relaxation after a hard day. Try the visualization technique and see how it affects your energy levels.

Caution: *avoid during pregnancy.*

INGREDIENTS

I cup dried sage	3 drops essential oil of lavender
I cup dried camomile flowers	3 drops essential oil of geranium
square of muslin and twine to tie	3 drops essential oil of camomile

1 Pile the herbs in the center of the muslin, then tie to secure.

2 Run a very warm bath, hanging the muslin bag beneath the hot faucet. Let it float in the water for at least 10 minutes.

3 Before stepping in, remove the bag and set aside to dry for another bath. Drop the essential oils into the water and swish to disperse.

4 Relax for 20 minutes or more, topping up the hot water as it cools.

5 Close your eyes and imagine a blue-white ball of light hovering above the crown of your head. Imagine the light slowly seeping down your body: over your head and shoulders, chest and arms, abdomen and legs, and down to your toes, filling you with a sense of calm, energy, and peace.

Relaxing listening

These are some of my favorite sounds for lengthy luxuriation in a warm bath. They should be available from good music stores or websites.

Turkish Woman at the Baths Pete LaRoca (32.Jazz): what more perfect title? Blissful modal jazz from the late 1960s.

East of the River Nile Augustus Pablo (Jetstar): Eastern-tinged reggae from the king of the melodica.

Hanging Gardens The Necks (Milk of Fish): Australian acoustic modern jazz that spins out a minimalist ceremony to accompany the longest of bathing rituals.

In a Silent Way Miles Davis (Sony Jazz): perhaps the most sensually seductive of all his electronic works; ever-mutating, moody, and surprisingly singalong soundscapes.

Ladies and Gentlemen We Are Floating in Space Spiritualized (Dedicated): relax and float away on ethereal, gospel-tinged guitar noise.

Tabula Rasa Arvo Pärt (ECM): easy-listening minimalism to transport you with glorious melodies and heavenly harmonies.

La Mer Debussy (numerous recordings): elemental impressionistic symphony, or "seascape without figures" as the composer dubbed it.

Blue Light 'Til Dawn Cassandra Wilson (Blue Note): heartfelt blues from an inventive jazz vocalist for late-night crooning sessions.

Blue Lines Massive Attack (Wild Bunch): the original and best chillout; music to take you up and down again.

Japanese hot soak

After thoroughly cleansing every inch of the body with a shower scrub (see page 51), Japanese bathers retire to a hot-water bath—and the hotter, the better—for a minimum of 30 minutes. Hot baths have a relaxing effect on the body because they cause blood to move away from the internal organs out to the extremities, slowing body systems. Deep heat draws away the lactic acid that gives rise to aching muscles, and eases joint pain. The perspiration that results generates a fantastic sensation of deep-down cleanliness. Intense heat also lulls the mind into a state of languid reflection. Most Western hydrotherapy practitioners would not recommend spending more than 15 minutes in a very hot bath, however, and you may feel more comfortable with a cool, wet washcloth on your brow. In Japan bathers might visit the *sento*, neighborhood communal bathhouse, of an evening for a hot soak, relaxation, and gossip; it makes sense to take such sedating baths after work and before bed.

AMERICANS BATHE TO GET CLEAN; JAPANESE CLEAN TO BATHE.

Traditional saying

Mineral bathing

Japan is reputed to have 10,000 *onsen*, volcanic sites where naturally heated water rises to the earth's surface. They are places of pilgrimage—many Japanese families plan their yearly vacations to incorporate a visit to a favorite hot-spring resort, and the numbers finding solace and peace this way have boomed since the 1980s. In a Shinto culture in which cleansing the body is synonymous with ridding mind and soul of impurities, *onsen* have a spiritual charge that derives from thousands of years' ritual cleansing, reverence, and healing. This is then only heightened by the setting of open-air *rotenburo* baths, literally "a bath amid the dew under an open sky." Bathers in these amazingly breathtaking natural springs can contemplate mountains and pine trees, rocks and seascapes, sky and moving trees as they rest in the hot water. The minerals in natural onsen water are credited with curative powers, and you can buy bags of mineral salts from many of the sites to add to home baths. Sodium chloride eases muscular tension, for example, and sulfur has an antiseptic effect, good for relieving skin problems. Legend has it that monks were first made aware of the curative powers of this mineral water by watching injured animals come to the water for healing.

Mineral salt bath

Adding mineral salts to a bath replicates the benefits of bathing in natural mineral springs. Shake a sachet into a tepid bath, or use as directed on the packet. Feel muscles give up tension as you relax in the water for 10 minutes, topping up with hot water until comfortably heated. Splash your face to tone the skin, then shower away any residue.

Caution: *avoid using mineral salts during pregnancy.*

Must-find salts

DEAD SEA SALTS: these contain a salt concentration ten times higher than regular sea salt. The unique mix of magnesium, potassium, calcium chlorides, and bromides leaves the skin silky-soft.

JAPANESE ONSEN SALTS: each hot spring that dots the Japanese islands has a different mineral combination. Look for the Tabi No Yado brand, salts from Atami or Nagano, and Meito Umi from the Beppu region of Kyushu island. Search also for salts blended to replicate the water at Kusatu, Hakone, Shirahama, and Shirabone.

EPSOM SALTS: formed from magnesium sulfate, these salts are fêted for their detoxifying action and ability to ease aches and pains.

The Dead Sea cannot be praised too highly…travelers take this salt home because it heals the human body.

Flavius Josephus

Warming winter bath

Ginger has a warming effect that suits it to winter bathing. In Japan ginger is combined with mandarin orange in baths to guard against winter colds; since medieval times in Europe, oranges have been studded with cloves to create pomanders that cleanse and scent the air and lift midwinter spirits. Both traditions meet in this bath.

Caution: *avoid during pregnancy.*

INGREDIENTS

grated zest of 2 mandarin oranges
1in (2.5cm) fresh ginger root, finely chopped

5 cloves, crushed
square of muslin and twine to tie

1 Heat the bathroom. Pile the fresh ingredients and cloves in the center of the muslin, then tie to secure.

2 Run a very warm bath, hanging the muslin bag beneath the hot faucet. Mix a warming massage oil in a dark glass bottle using 2 tbsp sweet almond oil, 4 drops each essential oils of petitgrain and neroli, and 2 drops essential oil of ginger, and stand in hot water to warm.

3 Relax in the bath for 20 minutes, letting the aromas lift the winter blues.

4 Pat yourself dry. While the skin is moist, massage vigorously with the oil.

Meditation bath

Switch off and tune out in this bath for complete mental shutdown and inner peace. Alternatively, take a Japanese-style meditation shower that replicates the *utesayo*, "let it beat water," experience beneath a natural waterfall. As you stand under a power shower, imagine a force of natural water beating down in an invigorating head massage.

INGREDIENTS

sandalwood incense : candles

1 Light the incense and candles. Step into a warm bath. Close your eyes and release tension in your toes and hands, lower back, neck, shoulders, and jaw.

2 Start to watch your breathing. Feel your in- and out-breaths slow and deepen as you relax. Imagine tension and toxins being exhaled with the out-breath; allow the in-breath to come naturally.

3 Draw your mind away from emotions that preoccupied you before you climbed into the bath.

4 Ask your brain to stop chattering. Imagine your mind as a blank screen, and watch thoughts pass over it then fade away again.

5 When you find yourself following a train of thought, step back, and wait for the screen to go blank again.

6 After a few minutes, open your eyes, wiggle your fingers and toes, and take time to come to before washing.

Candlelit bath

Bathing by candlelight is one of the joys of dark winter evenings. Candlemas, on February 2, is a particularly appropriate time to do so, since it comes during the part of the solar year between midwinter and the spring equinox associated in Celtic tradition with cleansing the body and home. Mark this time of new beginnings with a special candlelit bath using the yoga *trataka* candle-gazing meditation.

INGREDIENTS

nightlights,
sweet-scented beeswax,

tall church candles,
or floating flowerlights

1 While running a warm bath, fill the bathroom with candles. Site them away from towels and flammable products. Select a special candle and place it at the end of the bath.

2 Step into the bath. Relax for a while, then start to focus on the candle at the end of the bath. Focus your gaze on the tip of the flame, at the point at which its form and color disappear.

3 Keep your gaze steadily on the flame for up to a minute, trying not to blink, and breathing slowly and deeply.

4 Close your eyes and visualize the flame. When the image fades, open your eyes, and repeat the gaze. As thoughts intrude, let them just burn away and return your focus to the flame. Continue for 3 minutes or so. Never leave burning candles unattended.

Bedtime bath

Perfect for insomniacs, a warm bedtime bath shuts down the senses, eases muscular tension, and has a sedative effect on the mind. Make sure that you can emerge from the bath directly into freshly laundered bedlinen (in winter pop a hot-water bottle between the sheets before running the bath).

Caution: *omit marjoram oil during pregnancy and camomile and lavender in the first trimester.*

 **INGREDIENTS**

3 drops essential oil of camomile
2 drops essential oil of marjoram

2 drops essential oil of lavender

1 Run a very warm, deep bath. Just before stepping in, drop the essential oils into the water and swish to disperse.

2 Relax for 20 minutes or more with a calming book.

3 When you feel your eyes closing, pat yourself dry and head for bed. Before you hit the pillow, place 2 drops of lavender oil on the edge of the pillowcase. Alternatively, apply the oil to a tissue and place on the pillow.

Baby bathtime
Bathe babies in early evening, heating 2 drops of essential oil of lavender in water in an oil vaporizer to scent the room. Follow with a calming massage using a little sweet almond oil. Spritz the nursery with 2 drops of lavender oil in water in an atomizer.

Wake-up bath

Relaxing is all very well, but there comes a time when you need to inject some adrenaline to help you get up and go. Try these energizing cool baths to stir you up for work or refresh your brain on a hot, muggy day. Cold water seems to kickstart the immune system. A study at London's Thrombosis Research Institute reported that after exposure to cold water, participants had more disease-fighting white blood cells. Just 30 seconds under a cold shower suffices when you need instant energy: turn down the temperature gauge gradually.

Caution: *omit rosemary, basil, geranium, and juniper oils during pregnancy, rosemary if you have high blood pressure or epilepsy, and juniper if you have kidney disease.*

INGREDIENTS

Alarm-call oil blend:
4 drops essential oil of rosemary
3 drops essential oil of mandarin
2 drops essential oil of basil

Refreshing oil blend:
4 drops essential oil of grapefruit
3 drops essential oil of geranium
2 drops essential oil of juniper

1 Run a cool bath. Before stepping in, swish in one of the oil blends.

2 Relax for 5 minutes. Practice a version of alternate-nostril breathing (see page 56) using the stimulating right nostril only.

3 Turn on the cold faucet—make the bath as cool as you dare—and remain in it for 30 seconds.

4 Jump out of the bathtub and rub yourself dry briskly with a waffle towel.

APHRODISIAC BATHS

Steamy hot tubs in the open air, bubble baths for two, sensuous showers: water is made for loving play. Add to the mix essential oils, floral essences, and spices associated with seduction, and you have the perfect recipe for passion. Here are baths to share with a lover and sensuous massage ideas to follow on. Let them put you in the mood for love.

PERFECT KNOWLEDGE CAN ONLY BE ATTAINED
WHILE ONE IS ENJOYING THE PLEASURES OF
THE SENSES.

Saraha, *Tantric Buddhist master*

Fizzing champagne bath

Prepare for that big date by sinking into a big fizzing bath with a glass of something decadently sparkling. This champagne cocktail, invented for a Manhattan bartenders' competition in 1889, has become timeless. And once the bottle is open, who knows what might happen later....

 **INGREDIENTS**

3 tbsp baking soda
2 tbsp citric acid
1/2 tbsp cornstarch

3 drops essential oil of ylang ylang
3 drops essential oil of petitgrain
champagne cocktail (see below)

1 Run a warm bath. Mix the baking soda, citric acid, and cornstarch.

2 Mix a champagne cocktail to sip in the bath: place 1 sugar cube in a champagne flute and drop 2 dashes Angostura bitters on top. Pour over 2cl Cognac, then fill with champagne. Garnish with a twist of orange.

3 Before stepping into the bath, add the soda mixture, then drop the essential oils into the water and swish to disperse.

4 Sink into the fizzing bath and sip the cocktail. Feel yourself bubbling with evanescence, and let that set your mood for the evening.

Milk and honey bath

Cleopatra, the courtesans of the palaces of central Java, and Mughal queens alike are famous for their devotion to the softening, passion-preparing effects of milk on the skin. To seduce lovers Cleopatra is said to have spiced her surroundings with opiate-like scents and precious perfumed unguents. Follow the great queen's example, and, after bathing in milk, anoint the body with aromatic oils (she had handmaidens do this for her).

Caution: *omit jasmine oil during pregnancy.*

 INGREDIENTS

6 tbsp powder milk
3 tbsp runny honey

3 drops essential oil of sandalwood
3 drops essential oil of clary sage

1 Mix the powder milk and honey to make a stiff paste, then moisten with 2 cups of water; drop in the essential oils.

2 Mix a sensuous oil blend in a dark glass bottle using 2 tbsp sweet almond oil and 2 drops each of essential oils of sandalwood, jasmine, and patchouli. Stand the bottle in a basin of warm water.

3 Run a warm bath, stirring the scented paste in well before stepping in. Wallow in the milky water.

4 Pat yourself dry, then massage the sensuous oil blend into damp skin. Don a bathrobe and retire to bed.

Eastern wedding bath

Rose petals are scattered at a Christian wedding as a symbol of purity and love, while they blanketed Roman banquets so thickly that guests swooned. Across Asia, intoxicating perfumed flowers are cast into baths and beds for a wedding. An Indonesian marriage bed is seductively scented with pink, yellow, and mauve ylang ylang (literally "flower of flowers"). The blooms of this native Filipino tree yield such a heady scent that it is named the perfume tree, or crown of the East, and its essential oil is said to generate confident passion. It is irreplaceable in a sensuous bath oil. Purple-tinged white patchouli flowers have an intensely sweet muskiness that lingers. The oil has a history of use as an aphrodisiac and antidepressant for its ability to lift the spirits.

Caution: *omit rose oil during pregnancy.*

INGREDIENTS

3 drops essential oil of rose
3 drops essential oil of ylang ylang
3 drops essential oil of patchouli

2 tbsp sweet almond oil
handfuls of rose petals (fresh or dried)

1 Mix the essential oils into the sweet almond oil. Run a warm, deep bath.

2 Just before stepping in, pour the oil blend into the water and swish to disperse, then strew the rose petals over the bathwater.

3 Relax in the petal bath, swooning among the floral aromas.

Spicy seduction bath

Aphrodisiac powers have always been claimed for spices. Cardamom enjoyed a reputation in Ancient Egypt, Greece, and Rome as a love tonic. Cloves formed part of Indian love potions, while sandalwood, the most aphrodisiac of scents, is used by aromatherapists to release tension accompanying sexual problems. Follow this spice-infused bath by giving your partner a massage with a traditional blend of virility-boosting oils.

Caution: *omit cinnamon and rosemary oils during pregnancy, and rosemary oil if you have high blood pressure or epilepsy.*

INGREDIENTS

1 tsp cardamom pods, crushed	1 tsp black peppercorns
1 tsp cloves	square of muslin and twine to tie
1 tsp coriander seeds	8 drops essential oil of sandalwood

1 Crush the spices using a pestle and mortar and heat in a dry frying pan. Pile in the center of the muslin; tie to secure.

2 Mix a virility massage oil using 2 tbsp sweet almond oil, 4 drops essential oil of ginger, 3 drops essential oil of coriander, 2 drops essential oil of rosemary, and 1 drop essential oil of cinnamon leaf.

3 Run a warm bath, hanging the muslin bag beneath the hot faucet. Just before entering, swish in the sandalwood oil.

4 Relax in the bath, then pat yourself dry. Retire to bed for massage with the virility blend.

Bubble bath for two

Fill the tub with bubbles and squeeze up to indulge in this vanilla-scented bath. Because of its expense and rarity, vanilla was considered an aphrodisiac by the Aztecs. You might like to take a tub of the finest vanilla ice cream, and two long spoons, in with you. Follow with a silk dusting powder with the almost narcotic scent of jasmine, prized in Asia for its ability to evoke both passion and compassion.

Caution: *omit jasmine oil during pregnancy.*

INGREDIENTS

1 tbsp unscented bubble bath
2 tsp vanilla essence

large tub of vanilla ice cream

1 Run a warm, deep bath, adding the bubble bath and vanilla essence.

2 Make some silk dusting powder by spooning 4 tbsp cornstarch into a flour shaker. Drop in 8 drops essential oil of jasmine and secure the lid.

3 Climb into the bath and feed each other the ice cream.

4 Dry your partner, then dust your partner's body with a shaking of the powder and massage in well, feeling the scented cornstarch slide and slip over the skin. Retire to bed together.

Resources

Inspiring bathtime reads

CATHEDRALS OF THE FLESH: MY SEARCH FOR THE PERFECT BATH, Alexia Brue, London 2003, Bloomsbury

SOME LIKE IT HOT: THE SAUNA, ITS LORE AND STORIES, Nicolyn Rajala, Minnesota 2000, North Star Press of St. Cloud, Inc.

SPIRITUAL BATHING: HEALING RITUALS AND TRADITIONS FROM AROUND THE WORLD, Rosita Arvigo and Nadine Epstein, Berkeley CA 2003, Celestial Arts

THE HEALING ENERGIES OF WATER, Charlie Ryrie, London 1998, Gaia

UNDESIGNING THE BATH, Leonard Koren, Berkeley CA 1996, Stone Bridge Press

Great bath shopping

HAMMAM ACCESSORIES

www.HasanSoyer.com for hammam sets, bowls and clogs, *kese* hand mitts and pumice stones, natural soaps and towels

JAPANESE BATHING PRODUCTS

www.naturaljapanesebeauty.com for onsen salts blended to replicate the waters at the resorts of Kusatu, Hakone, Shirahama, and Shirabone

www.itmonline.org for Meito Umi onsen salts

www.fastriver.com a Canadian online onsen guide selling Tabi No Yado, or "Traveller's Inn," bath powders

Picture credits